JUN 0 8

FEATHERS AND FUR

Mel Higginson

Rourke

Publishing LLC

Vero Beach, Florida 32964

www.rourkepublishing.com

PHOTO CREDITS: All photos © Lynn M. Stone

Title page: In cold places, the tiger grows a thick fur coat.

Editor: Robert Stengard-Olliges

Cover design by Nicola Stratford.

Library of Congress Cataloging-in-Publication Data

Higginson, Mel.
 Feathers and fur / Mel Higginson.
    p. cm. — (Let's look at animals)
 Includes index.
 ISBN 1-60044-171-8 (Hardcover)
 ISBN 1-59515-530-9 (Softcover)
 1. Fur—Juvenile literature. 2. Feathers—Juvenile literature. I. Title.
II. Series: Higginson, Mel. Let's look at animals.
 QL942.S737 2007
 599.7'147—dc22
                                   2006012748

Printed in the USA

CG/CG

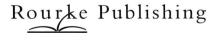

Rourke Publishing

www.rourkepublishing.com – sales@rourkepublishing.com
Post Office Box 3328, Vero Beach, FL 32964

Table of Contents

Mammals

Skin and some hair cover your body. Many other animals are covered by skin and hair, too. All animals with true hair are called **mammals**.

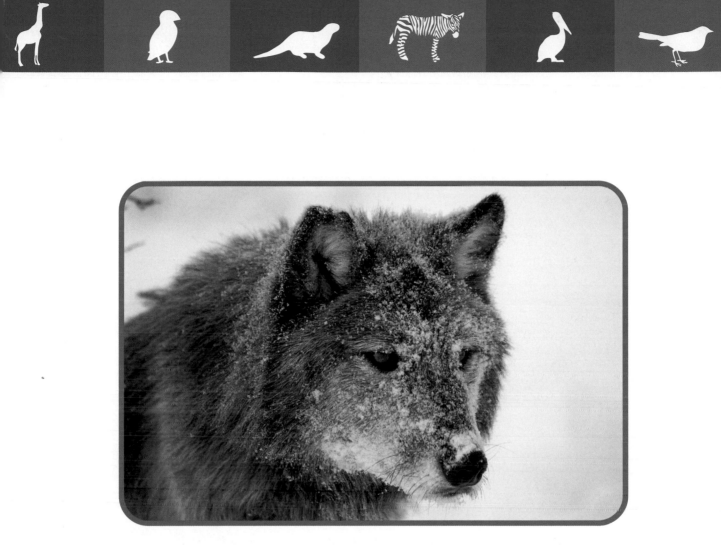

Hair grows from a mammal's skin. Most mammals are covered by hair. A wolf is a mammal covered with hair.

Soft or Stiff

Foxes have a coat of thick, soft hair. The thick, soft hair of some wild animals is called fur.

A raccoon's soft fur comes in many colors. Not a fur is the same.

Many mammal coats have stiff outer hairs. The long outer hairs of the Wolverine's coat are guard hairs.

Porcupine's quills are special guard hairs. They are stiff and sharp.

Fur

A coat usually has thick **underfur,** too. Sea otters have the thickest fur. Sea otters must clean their coats often to keep them waterproof.

A sea otter uses its paws and claws to keep its fur clean.

Fur helps keep a mammal dry, like a raincoat. Fur helps keep a mammal warm, like a blanket. The color of fur helps an animal hide.

Bears dry themselves by shaking water from their outer coat.

Feathers

Skin and feathers cover birds' bodies. Some kinds of birds even have feathers on their legs and feet.

Like hairs, feathers grow upward from skin. Birds have two main kinds of feathers. **Contour feathers** are large. **Down** feathers are small and fluffy.

Feathers are Useful

A feather has a long center "post" called a **shaft**. The wide, colorful part of a feather is the **vane**.

Feathers help a bird stay cool or warm. They protect the bird's skin. The feathers and fat of penguins keep them warm!

Feathers also help a bird fly. Feathers make wings larger and keep them lightweight.

The colors of feathers are important. Feather colors
can help a bird hide. They can help a bird find a **mate**.

Feathers wear out. Most birds shed old feathers. Feathers do not fall out all at once. New feathers replace the old.

Glossary

contour feathers (KION toor feth ur) — a bird's outer and larger feathers

down (DOUN) — the soft, fuzzy feathers under a bird's contour feathers

mammal (MAM uhl) — an animal that makes mother's milk and grows hair

mate (MATE) — an adult animal's adult partner or partners

shaft (SHAFT) — the long center rod of a feather

underfur (UHN dur fur) — the thick coat of fur against the skin of some mammals

vane (VAYN) — the tiny strands that reach out together from a feather shaft; the wide part of a feather

Index

FURTHER READING

Miles, Elizabeth. *Fur and Feathers*. Heinemann, 2002.

Twist, Clint. *Furry Creatures.* Waterbird Books, 2005.

WEBSITES TO VISIT

http://www.findarticles.com/p/articles/mi_m0EPG/is_n7_v31/a:_19563010

http://www.edhelper.com/AnimalReadingComprehension_1_1.html

http://www.kidzone.ws/animals/birds.html

ABOUT THE AUTHOR

Mel Higginson writes children's nonfiction and poetry. This is Mel's first year writing for Rourke Publishing. Mel lives with his family just outside of Tucson, Arizona.